CONTENTS KU-778-562

Knot for the Faint of Heart

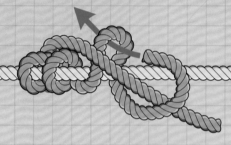

Knots. It's easy to take the little guys and gals for granted. You need one thing attached to another. Well, let's see… I'll just twist this piece of rope…over this piece of rope. Nope. You need proper Knot Knowledge. And, friend, you've come to the right place.

Knowing how to tie things together properly is more than just a skill. It's a magic trick and a super power combined in a little bundle. Luckily, what is true of knots is true of nearly everything in life: if you practice, you'll get better at it.

So read the book. And the next time you're adrift at sea or facing a menacing bear, with a piece of rope in your pocket, you'll be the one who can save the day.

Knot Talk
A basic glossary

Here's a selection of basic knot lingo for the would-be lion hunter, mountain conqueror, camping guru, or peg-legged boat captain.

The bight is a curve or arc, often caused by slack. It is not to be confused with a loop: the critical difference is that the two sections of rope have not crossed, but are next to each other.

The loop is just that—a loop in the rope, wherein the ends of the rope cross over each other and a circle is created.

A turn is where a rope wraps around another object 360 degrees. We'll talk about turns a lot in this book.

Working end

Standing rope

Ends are the ends of the rope.

Standing rope is the unused part.

The **working end** is the opposite end from the standing rope—the part you're using to tie the knot.

There are limitless knots, but they fall into a very small number of categories:

Hitches fasten ropes to objects, such as bear's legs or (rather more mundanely) tent poles.

Bends unite two rope ends, despite their differences.

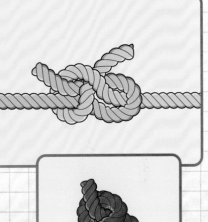

Stoppers stop stuff, like the rope (or another rope) from traveling or fraying.

Finally, **decorative knots** are very pretty!

Tips for the First-time Knot Tier

(knot basics)

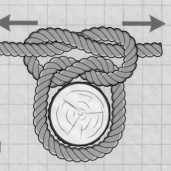

Whether you are attempting to trap a wild bear, setting up a trip wire to trap some poachers, or just making camp in the woods, there are some basic skills that should be in the arsenal of every aspiring knot specialist.

Much of what follows seems simple, but all knots benefit from being pulled apart, both literally and figuratively. The most rudimentary are the building blocks for the rest, or in some cases are examples of stumbling blocks that are mastered in order to be properly cast aside.

Since they count as basic rope skills, a few techniques for caring for your ropes have been included here.

Basic Overhand (or Thumb Knot) and Double Overhand

A knot that's a good place to start

When learning to tie knots, it's smart to begin at the beginning, often with the most basic of ideas. Like the simple song of adventure that all sailors, hikers, and climbers hear, calling them to action, there is one knot that we all just sort of know when a rope is put into our hands.

The Overhand is truly the most basic thing you can do with a rope in your hand. Although it is useful as a stopper, Ashley's Stopper Knot (Lesson 16) is the best choice for that, and the Figure 8 (Lesson 3) is better, and easy and pretty, too. The Basic Overhand is most practically used as a quick way to prevent the end of your rope from fraying.

The first knot in the book and it's one you already know how to do! See, it's easy this knot business.

1 Form a loop in the rope.

2 Pass the rope end through the loop.

3 Tighten it to form the Overhand knot. It's a simple stopper knot! Verrrrry simple indeed.

4 To form a Double Overhand instead, pass the end through the loop twice in step 2 above and pull tight, forming a larger stopper knot. It's better than the Basic Overhand, but still not great.

Half Hitch

A knot that loves company

Moments of haste occur in all knot-masters' lives. This will work if you need to secure your trusty horse, boat, dog, or bicycle in a hurry, but it will lead to their inevitable theft or escape, so don't rely on it too heavily.

✳ While the Half Hitch can be used by itself, it shouldn't be. It's basically what you do if you have a rope and you put it around something. It is best used to increase the security of a primary knot, or in addition to other knots.

1 Loop the rope once around an object such as a tree, a pole, or a friend's leg. Pass the rope over the standing end, and pass it through the loop.

2 For extra security, pass the rope around the standing end.

3 Pass the rope through itself and tighten again to create a second half hitch.

Figure 8 Stopper Knot
A knot to put a stop to things

So you need a stopper knot, but you want to make sure that the horse you're securing to the post outside of the Wayside Inn is properly impressed by its aesthetics? With finesse and aplomb, we proudly present the tried and true Figure 8 Stopper Knot for your consideration and perusal, Mr. Horse. But be mindful that if your horse is fussy, it might pull it undone and follow you into the inn for a refreshing glass of water and a carrot.

A favorite amongst boaters, the Figure 8 is a reliable stopper knot, certainly better than the Basic Overhand, and elegant, too. It's easy to tie and doesn't tend to bind. However, with the wrong tug it can just as easily unbind, so don't use it in hope of ultimate security.

1 Form a loop by passing the tail over itself. Keep the loop open, and pass the rope under and then back around its standing end.

2 Now bring the tail back through that open loop, and you should have a nice little "8" shape. Pull it tight—it's quite satisfying.

Figure 8 stopper knot   13

Half Knot

A knot you already know

Even before you were a knot-master with ropes and twines coloring your bespeckled eyes, when a rope was put into your hand, you felt the urge to tie a good knot. And if you didn't tie an overhand, you tied a half knot. But was it good for anything? Well, no, not much, but it's easy, so it's worth noting if only to have it in your vocabulary.

The Half Knot is unreliable for more than a quick fix. Repeating the knot and then finishing it with a Square Knot (Lesson 5) can be sufficient for many small loads, but is still unreliable. Keep reading!

1 Cross the rope over itself and pass one end back under itself.

2 Pull tight around the intended load-taking object.

Square Knot (Reef Knot)

A Knot all Scouts Should Know

The Half Knot leads us squarely to its distinguished elder brother: the Square or Reef Knot. You've gotten so good at tying things up that you are now steps ahead of your knot-tying buddy. So you tie him up, knowing full well that with a bit of fussing he'll escape the Square Knot.

✳ It should be noted that as with the Half Knot, the Square Knot is unreliable at best. That said, it is perfectly viable in any situation where safety is not paramount, from tying up bundles of sacred scrolls to lacing your trusty adventurer's boot.

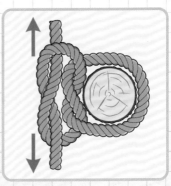

1 Following the steps in Lesson 4, form up a half knot with style and aplomb. Now cross the ropes over and under again.

2 Pull the loop tight.

✳ Lessons 4 and 5 have effectively codified the easiest knots ever, and perhaps the most common.

Rope Coiling

Not a knot, but one for clean freaks

You climbed Mount Magnus, took a selfie to prove you'd made it, and shared it on Instagram with your climber friends. But now it's time to give yourself and your rope some hard-earned rest. This mighty rope has served you well on your long journey, but it's both lazy and an inanimate object, so it's not going to coil itself.

✳ A well-coiled rope is a good and proud thing. It will be easier to use the next time you need it, and ultimately it'll last longer. The secret is to alternate the coils and to follow the natural coil of the rope (pro tip: this works for wiring, too). Once you've begun coiling it poorly, the rope will "remember," and will flop about and bend in an annoying fashion for the rest of its time with you. That makes proper rope people hurt inside, and it leads to tangled lines and unhappy ropes. Heavier ropes can require different coiling techniques (such as passing it behind your back to take the weight), but most are based on the following principle.

{ Treat your rope with a little love and it'll last you a good long time. }

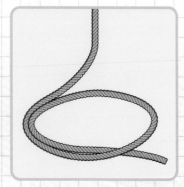

1 Start by making a coil (or circle) of rope in your hand to the size you want your full coil to be.

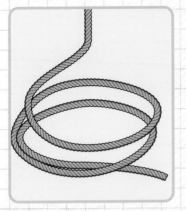

2 You are going to continue making coils of the same size, but alternate whether the rope goes over or under itself.

3 Continue going over and under until you have just enough line left to wrap the rope. As with many things in life, knowing where to stop coiling will take some experience. Much depends on how much rope you have in the first place. Try to leave about one loop's worth.

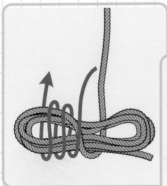

4 Now wrap the end of the rope around your established coil several times, covering the full body of the rope. It should be firmly wrapped, but not so tight that there is no longer room in the center of the coil.

5 Now pass the bight (see page 5) back through the center of the coil two or three times and pull it tight, adding a Half Hitch (Lesson 2) or Square Knot (Lesson 5) as a loose finish if you like.

Whipping the Rope
For those knot tiers with OCD

You had to divide your one coil of rope between yourself, a park ranger, and a surly old cowboy. If you don't whip the freshly cut ends, your trusty rope will surely fray, leaving you and your rag-tag group stranded at the bottom of this gorge. And nobody wants to be stranded for twelve hours with a grouchy cowboy telling stories about his favorite horse.

✸ Whipping rope (not to be confused with making a whip out of rope, Indiana!) is essential to rope care, and not too difficult if you have a little twine in hand. A more advanced and secure whipping, the Sailmaker's Whipping, uses a similar technique with a needle and thread. Look it up if you want to get fancy at your dinner party.

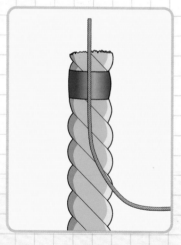

Do not confuse with whipping with ropes!

1 If possible, secure the loose end of the rope temporarily with tape or a short tie. In a pinch, wet it. Lay the twine in a single line on to the rope. The long end of the twine should be heading away from the frayed end of the rope.

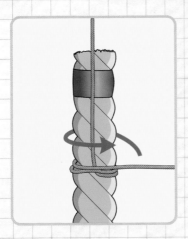

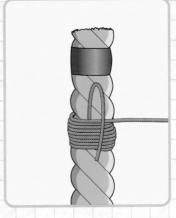

2 Wrap the long end back around the standing twine eight to ten times in even and tight rows, heading toward the frayed end.

3 Now make a bight (see page 5) out of the short end of the twine, and pass it back over the wrapped rows.

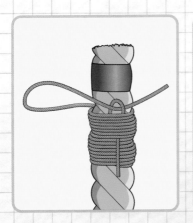

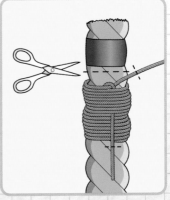

4 Now wrap a further eight to ten even and tight rows, this time wrapping over the formed bight. Be careful not to wrap over the loop of the bight, as you will need that. On the last turn, pull the rope through the bight.

5 Pull the short end and futz it around a bit, hiding and securing each end, then trim. Nice rope!

Whipping the rope

A Sailor's Knots of the Sea

(Nautical knots)

Your knot quest has inevitably led you to the ferocious and fair open sea. This last great frontier is home to an endless menagerie of pirates and other scallywags, sea creatures, and their kin. And there's no way to survive Neptune's wrath without a supply of staunch rope and the know-how to tie it.

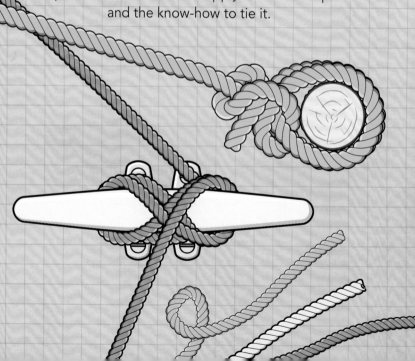

Sheet Bend

A knot for tying two tentacles together

Picture the scene: you've tracked a giant squid and have him pinned against Dead Man's Reef. But he's as quick as he is beautiful. In the blink of an eye his fearsome tentacles are upon you like a slimy hammer in the night. But your instincts hold true, good captain, as you have just the thing for tying two medium-size squid tentacles together in a hurry.

This hitch works best if you have ropes (or tentacles) of different thicknesses. It is fast to tie, and an improvement on the Square Knot (Lesson 5) in almost every way. Many discerning knot-smiths (Ashley amongst them) consider this to be one of the essential knots to have at your disposal.

Amazingly, some people don't have easy access to tentacles. In that case, rope will do.

1 Start with two ropes, ideally of different thicknesses (although the same thickness will work). Form a loose bight (see page 5) at the end of the thicker rope. Pass the thinner rope through the bight.

2 Now pass the thinner rope under the two parallel ropes that form the bight.

3 Finally, pass the thin rope back under itself and pull tight.

Double Sheet Bend
A knot to join two ropes together

Your boat has sunk. You are lost at sea and trying to keep your head above water. You sense a movement in the darkness. A lidded eye the size of your boat itself stirs open, and stares at you. A sea beast that defies all logic lurches toward you. You're going to need a bigger knot.

✳ The Double Sheet Bend is just like the Sheet Bend (Lesson 8), but with more turns. It's sturdier, and good for larger ropes, but it's worth noting separately, particularly if your two ropes are of drastically different sizes.

1 Follow the steps for the Sheet Bend (Lesson 8), but in step 2 pass the thinner rope under the two parallel ropes that form the bight and wrap twice instead of once. Finish by passing the thin rope back under itself and pulling tight.

{ Does double the sheet bend mean double the fun? No, but it's a useful knot to know. }

Slip Knot and Noose

A knot for practical jokers

You've been at sea for a few weeks, and the crew members are starting to get restless. Practical jokes have started, and First Mate Barry just glued your shoes to the deck…the swine. It's time for revenge! While Barry sleeps, you form a Slip Knot and attach it to the end of Barry's peg leg, then tie the other to his bunk. You scream "Fire! Fire!" and watch as Barry leaps up, tries to escape, and spills the entire contents of his drawers in the process. Take that Barry, ye peg-legged scurvy dog.

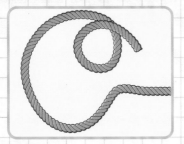

1 Make a large loop in the end of your rope. Using the end, make a smaller loop inside the larger loop.

2 Pull the larger loop back through the smaller. You should now have a loose knot, and a loop on the bight.

The Slip Knot is very close to its more nefarious cousin, the Hangman's Noose, and should never be tied around a human. It can alternately be used in the wild as an effective snare. Poor bunnies.

3 Loosen the larger bight so that it is big enough to bring around your intended object (a standing pole, for example), and pull it tight.

Cleat Hitch

A knot to fix your boat to a dock

You've amassed your sailing crew, a roguish gaggle of miscreants and sea-dogs, not one of them without at least one peg-leg, parrot, or eye-patch. It's almost as if they went shopping for outfits together... But even a band of sea-faring brigands must occasionally step off the boat and onto land, and for this you need the Cleat Hitch.

✳ This tie assumes that you have an actual cleat, which is the (generally metal) thingy (sorry for all the technical terms) that appears almost universally on proper docks and boats. This knot also assumes that you will have access to the most common of cleats, the horn cleat, named for the two metal arms on each side that look a bit like horns. We'll refer to the two arms as the near horn and the far horn, which is to say the one closer to where you are docking and the one farther, respectively.

These cleats come in as many sizes as there are sizes of boat.

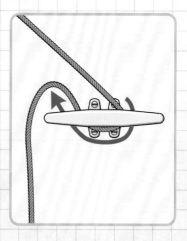

1 Begin by wrapping your rope around the far horn of the cleat, then back around the near horn, stopping the wrap before you cross the initial line fully.

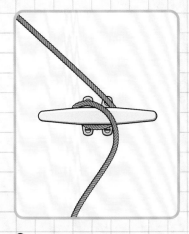

2 Bring the rope back up over the body of the cleat.

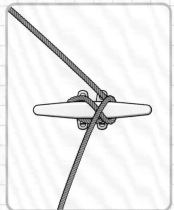

3 Wrap the rope back over itself so that it forms a loop around the far horn and passes back over the middle of the cleat.

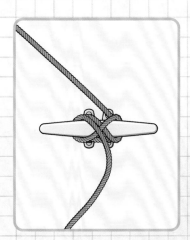

4 Send the rope back under and over the near cleat, passing back over the middle.

5 You are effectively tying figure eights around the cleat. The number of turns depends largely on the type of rope you are using and how likely it is to slip.

Marlinspike Hitch (Hoop)

A knot for saving drowning shuffleboard hooligans

Man overboard! An on-deck game of shuffleboard on the over-60s cruise has gotten a bit out of hand, and one guest has pushed another off the boat. You need to get him back, and fast. Take that rope and grab those paddles from those rioting seniors…it's time to make a rope ladder.

The Marlinspike Hitch, or Hoop, is an effective, quick, and simple way to set up a knot that grips and will take a decent amount of weight. It's very handy. If you really are making a ladder, you'll need to repeat the process in a parallel fashion, doing your utmost to keep the knots and poles running evenly. Although wonky ladders do have a certain pirate-fort charm…

> This hitch provides a super-fast and super-easy way to make a rope ladder.

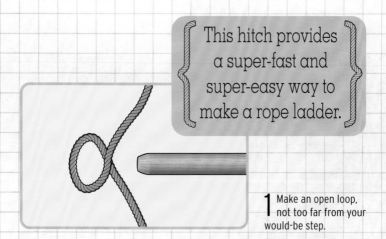

1 Make an open loop, not too far from your would-be step.

2 Now tuck a bight (see page 5) from the standing end back through the loop, still without tightening.

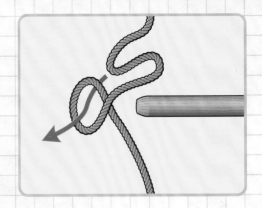

3 Bring the loop you formed with the bight over the would-be step, and pull it tight.

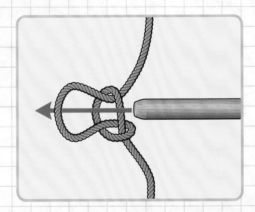

4 Repeat at the other end of the step with another rope, and continue the process for each step.

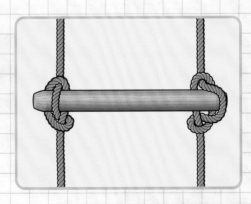

Albright Knot

A knot for catching fish

A genuine sea-dog requires near-constant sustenance in order to maintain the proper balance of surliness peppered with loudly yelled "ARRRRs!" Some fishing line and a spot to cast off are a must, but a respected sailor ought to be able to tie that line in order to catch the tastiest fish from the deep.

✳ Fishing and the ties associated with it are worth another building-full of books, but here's a good start. It's the first time we're tackling a trickier knot, and it might take a bit of practice, but it's very useful for tying thin lines together. If you're paying attention, it'll strike you as an advanced form of the indispensable Sheet Bend (Lesson 8), just with lots more turning.

1 Form an even and open loop in one of your lines, the thicker one if they are different. Pass the other line through the loop.

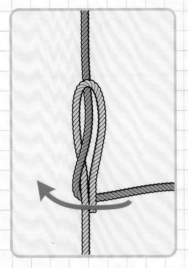

2 Bring the thinner rope behind the thicker, and wrap it nice and tightly back around itself.

3 Continue wrapping neatly and tightly toward the open end of the thinner rope. Depending on the lines, you should be able to wrap between 8 and 15 times—you're done when you still have a little bit of the first loop left, and a small end from the thinner line. It should be starting to look pretty smart, so keep those loops neat.

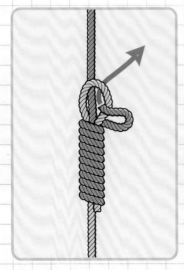

4 Now pass the thin end back through the remaining loop, keeping it running next to itself. To finish, pull both the thick and thin ends tight and trim if required.

Anchor Hitch (or Bend)

A knot to accompany a thousand hipster tattoos

The nautical life is rife with salty accouterments, such as mast, sail, and tiller. But there's one item that keeps you where you need to be in the midst of a storm. No, not the parrot. As the name implies (or in fact states directly), the Anchor Hitch is best used for holding a rope fast to any intimidating anchor, tattoos notwithstanding.

> *This is very effective for tying a rope to an anchor. It resembles your old friend the Half Hitch (Lesson 2) in many ways, and in point of fact, two half hitches combined would prrrrobably work just as well. But because this knot has the word "anchor" in it, it's inherently cooler.*

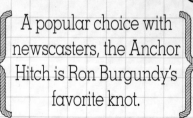

A popular choice with newscasters, the Anchor Hitch is Ron Burgundy's favorite knot.

1 Turn the rope around a post twice, but keep the turns loose.

2 Bring the tail over the standing rope and under the first loose turn. You've formed your old friend the Half Hitch (Lesson 2)! It's nice to see her again.

3 Now bring the rope end back around the starting end.

4 To finish, feed the end through the loop made in the previous step to make a second half hitch.

Double Fisherman's Knot

A knot that's not for fishing

The giant squid from Lesson 8 is back. When last you met, he straight-up ate your First Mate, threw a variety of perfectly good life jackets into the ocean, and knocked over your good candy jar. So this time it's personal. Like a streak of slimy lightning in the night, his enormous appendages are nearly upon you. A good dose of the Double Fisherman's Knot will make sure that they remain tied together. Forever.

This is an excellent and reliable knot, and the foundation for another important knot, the Prusik (Lesson 34). The only potential problem worth noting is that it is nearly impossible to untie (a good thing in the instance of the Prusik). And don't tell your fisherman friends, but the knot's rarely actually used in fishing—it's better suited to climbing.

1 Place the two lines parallel to each other. Bring one line over the second, then pass it back under both.

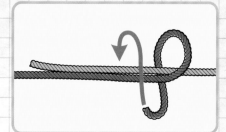

2 Wrap the line under once more, leaving open turns. Now pass this end through both open turns, and tighten.

3 Now repeat the process with the other rope, passing it under and wrapping twice.

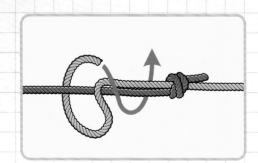

4 Pass the end through the turns, as before.

5 Pull on both ropes to tighten the knots and "marry" them.

Ashley's Stopper Knot
A knot to stop anything

Batten the hatches! A storm has been battering decks and hearts for nigh on four days, but it's about to reach fever pitch. Your rope is jammed up, and if you don't relieve the tension on the winch, the whole sail's going to let go. You can't let the Beige Bessie go down like that! You've got to clear that line, but a stopper is crucial to hold the tension at bay.

✴ Ashley's Stopper is named after the man himself, and is widely used and well-regarded. It's a fine stopper (and this author's personal favorite), although certain situations do demand others. It seems really simple, but it's oddly easy to mess up. Be careful when passing the loop under and through, and when tightening the half knot.

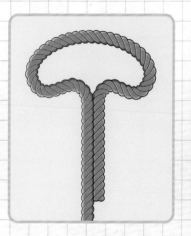

1 You're going to tie a half knot around your standing line. Form up a big bight (see page 5).

2 Now fold the bight down on itself, forming two loops.

3 Pass the loop from the standing end under and through the other loop, but don't tighten.

4 Now bring the tail through the remainder of the loop, not through the formed-up knot. You've now built the half knot around your standing line.

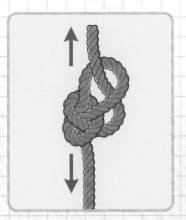

5 Tighten that half knot before the rest (this is particularly important to avoid slippage). Now pull the tail tight, and then the standing end tight, forming the knot up fully.

6 Here's a picture of the finished knot for reference.

The Outdoor Adventurer's Guide to Life in the Forest

(camping knots)

The meat and potatoes of a proper knot-lover's life inevitably take place in a forest. That's just how it goes. It's statistically proven that 74% of all Cub Scouts and 48% of all wannabe Bear Grylls, spend 59% of their lives in forests. And aside from your tent, flashlight (torch), and compass, there's nothing you need more than a well-coiled rope.

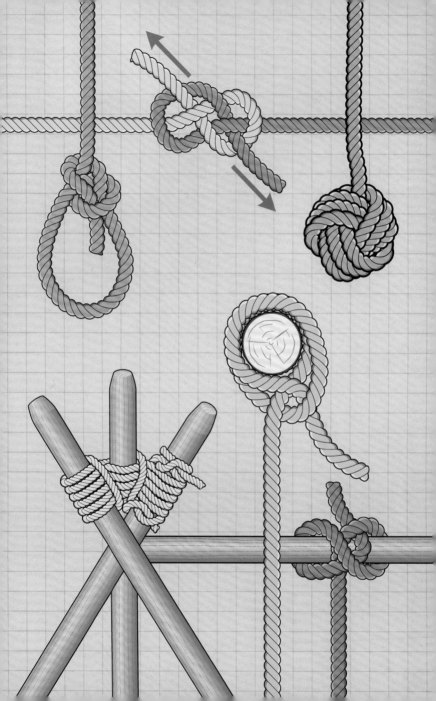

Bowline (Bowlan)

A knot to trip up poachers

The sun rises on day two of your intrepid quest. You ready your trusty horse, Carfax, breathe deeply in the morning air, and salute the rising sun. But something's not right. On the breeze you detect the bouquet of stale whiskey, tobacco smoke, and crime—the unmistakable stench of a party of poachers heading toward you. With little time to act, you use two trusty Bowlines to erect a quick trip wire.

✳ The Bowline is a very good knot for fastening a rope to any sort of post or other standing object, or to take a load. It's easy, and can even be done one-handed with practice (I'll time you!). The only disadvantage is that it's very difficult to let loose if it does have a load, but still, this is an essential knot to know.

1 Begin by making a little loop in the rope. Leave enough rope for the loop size that you want to have left over.

2 Pass the rope end through the loop as you would for an overhand knot.

3 Now continue sending the rope behind and all the way back around the standing end that is above your little loop. Now pull the end back through the small loop.

{ Making a trip wire? You better believe a big bowline is your best bet. }

One-handed variant:

A true outdoorsman can do things with only one hand, leaving the other free to tie, hoist, and build. Here's the one-handed version—it's tricky, but both possible and useful:

1 Make a loop around your hand while holding the short end of the rope.

2 Bring the short end around the standing end by wiggling your hand about a bit.

3 With the short end still in hand, wiggle your hand out of the mix.

Clove Hitch
A classic knot for hanging drapes

There's no way to cross the Double-fisted Chasm except by using Flanders' Passing. Unfortunately the land bridge is frequently closed, and today is no exception, because the end of the rope bridge has come loose. The quickest way to secure the rope to the post is definitely a Clove Hitch. But cross with caution: this knot can be unpredictable.

The Clove Hitch is a classic, but it should be used with a measure of caution. While some people consider it essential, we at the Knot Institute of Adventures find it unreliable in many situations. It is best used by those who like to live dangerously. Or for hanging drapes. In short, while it's good to know, don't use this knot if safety is paramount.

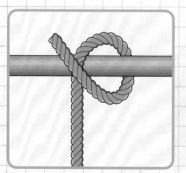

1 Wrap the rope end around a post and/or bow staff.

2 Wrap the rope back over the post in a figure eight.

3 Bring the working end under the last turn and pull tight.

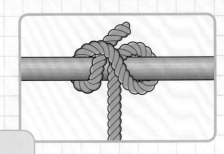

Variant:

Alternatively, this can be done with two loops, and with practice can be done very quickly:

1 Make one loop and put it over a post.

2 Follow it with a second loop of the same size from the slack at the working end.

3 Bring the second loop around the post and pull tight.

Monkey's Fist

A superficial knot to keep wild bears out of reach

That noise in the night was more than just the wind. It turns out that, yes, once again, you've managed to set up camp amidst a sleeping family of bears. And it's now approaching breakfast time. If you're going to get out of this one unscathed, you'll need to heave yourself up into a tree so the bears can't reach you. You'll need some heft to your rope, and that's where the Monkey's Fist comes in.

✳ Some say the Monkey's Fist is just for looking pretty. But it can indeed be useful as a so-called heave-line. Basically, it gives some weight to your line, especially with a weight tucked inside it. But most importantly, it has the best name of all the knots. This is a significant knot in your knot-tying experience. It's a little weird and convoluted and takes practice and dexterity. But you'll get it and then say, "I TIE KNOTS!" It'll be awesome. Monkey awesome.

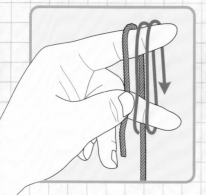

1 You're going to use your fingers as a base for the knot to wrap itself around.* Start by wrapping down around your fingers three times. Make sure to leave a decent amount of slack on the working end, as there will be a lot more wrapping.

* Here I've used my index and ring fingers. This leaves a gap that you can use as an alternative for step 2, as it offers some support when you wrap the rope around the loop.

2 At this juncture, remove your fingers, but try to keep the structure of the turns together in your hand.** Now wrap three more turns around the body of the first three turns.

** Some knot-smiths would have you bring through the middle here, but I prefer to wait until the next step to start securing.

3 Pass the working end around one of the full sets of turns. Now you should be starting to get the structure together. You're readying the body of the knot to pass back through the inside.

4 Wrap three times again through the center, back around the previous set of wraps. At this point you should have the makings of the "fist" in hand. Some people put a hard object inside in order to add weight, such as a ball bearing or a rock. Just don't swing it at your friend's head.

5 Finish with a simple Overhand (Lesson 1) and tuck it into the body.

6 Patiently tighten up each turn by feeding through loose loops and pulling the end of the rope.

Carrick Bend

A cool-looking knot for attaching ropes together

As tricky as it is high-performing, the Carrick is good for pulling two ropes together, although in a pinch it can be used to secure two ends of a rope together.

> This bend is another solid alternative to the Square Knot (Lesson 5), and it's easier to untie. Moreover, it's very pretty. Most of all, it's best suited for tying much larger ropes and cables together. So go do that.

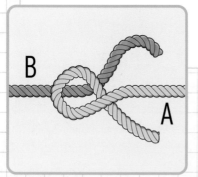

1 Take two ropes and form a small loop in one of them (rope A), making sure the tail passes under the standing end. Lay the loop on top of and across the working end of the other rope (rope B).

2 Assuming rope B begins in the "under" position, the following steps can be simplified by thinking of them as alternating over and under. So begin by bringing rope B over the standing end of rope A. Bring B under the very end of A.

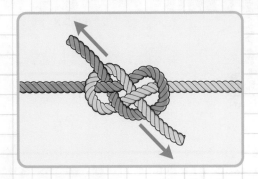

3 Now bring rope B back to the loop, going over A, and then back under itself. Bring it back over A and out of the loop. To finish, pull both standing ends tight.

LESSON 21

Poacher's Knot
Errr, a knot for poaching

An adventurer in the forest is sure to develop a powerful hunger. For capturing small, non-poisonous creatures, the Poacher's Knot is just the thing. Although if you capture that rabbit named Wilfred, it's best to set him free. He's a favorite of the park ranger, and eating him is no joke.

1 Form a bight (see page 5) in the end of the rope and loosely wrap the end around the bight twice.

2 Pass the end through the turns and pull tight.

Constrictor Knot
A knot for capturing snakes
(or, less excitingly, tying up bags)

So, how to use a Constrictor Knot... Let's say, for example, you find that some inconsiderate jerk has left his bag of boa constrictors untied. You may well ask, "What is he even doing with all those snakes?," and you'd be perfectly justified—if I saw a man carrying around a bag of giant snakes, I'd be slightly bemused, too—but bear with me. IF you did find four or five boa constrictors slithering out of a bag, the Constrictor Knot is coincidentally just the thing for closing up said bag.

1 Make a turn around the intended object, bringing the working end over the standing end.

2 Continue by bringing the working end behind the intended object.

3 Bring the working end over the standing rope and under the first turn. Pull firmly on the ends.

This knot does work well for tying up bags, and is actually quite handy to know.

Rolling Hitch
A knot for animal lovers

Your map was spot on, and nestled in the thicket just west of the old graveyard you find it: a herd of miniature horses. Shetland ponies, to be precise, complete with miniature saddles, miniature reins, and miniature riders. Well, not miniature riders, but you get the idea. It's all very cute, but they're shy creatures, so if you want to pet one you're going to have to tie it up. Good thing you learned the Rolling Hitch, my friend.

✳ The Rolling Hitch is good for use with smaller ropes, particularly when attaching them to larger ones. But it also has a variety of practical applications, for example as an effective stopper, or to take the strain off a winch. Its main drawback is that it doesn't work so well with modern, synthetic ropes, which tend to be a bit slippery.

1 Bring one rope around another to form your old friend the Half Hitch (Lesson 2). Keep going until you've gone around and over the first turn. Make sure the rope tucks between the standing end and the first turn. Pull this tight.

2 Now loop round again to form another half hitch.

Tautline Hitch
A knot for avoiding yogi and co

It's been a long day, knot traveler. You hiked up Vulture Mountain, trekked down Wolf Canyon, and took a detour to Coyote Gulch. The forest is clearly a hotbed of dangerous animals, so you should probably make a secure campsite before the sun goes down and the man-eating bears emerge. It's pretty well-known that in addition to wanting to eat you, bears have awful breath and a love of picnic baskets.

✳ The Tautline resembles its cousin the Rolling Hitch (Lesson 23), but is a favorite amongst campers for its ability to tighten or loosen easily, and then seize under a load. This makes it ideal for tent lines, although some argue that a Midshipman's Hitch is better. But I prefer this one, and I wrote the book, so take that.

1 Bring a turn around the post or spike. Wrap the working end around the standing end twice, going toward the post or spike.

2 Bring the working end of the rope under itself, working now away from the post. Make a third turn outside of the two existing turns.

3 Pass the end through the loop. Tighten the knot and slide it to adjust the tension.

Timber Hitch

A knot for campers and ukulele players

You've erected a pretty nice campsite (in classic Scout fashion) in the Lost Forest. Not too flashy, but not without style. This being the Lost Forest, which is to say the forest that people often get lost in, you're thinking you might stay a while. Now is the time for some added security!

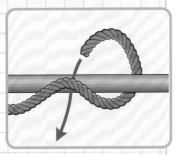

As the name implies, this is a knot that has long been used to attach rope to trees. Strictly speaking, it needs tension to be effective, but it is unlikely to jam or untie. Interestingly enough, it is also used to attach strings to some instruments, including the much-loved ukulele. Which is also welcome in any and all campsites…

1 Loop the rope around the pole and under the standing end.

2 Now bring it back over the standing end and through the loop you just made.

3 Make three more turns around the working part of the rope, against the pole. For stability and hauling you can add more half hitches farther down.

Square Lashing

A knot for house-proud campers

It looks as though your campsite may be even more permanent than your initial calculations suggested. Make sure the surrounding forest is both free from ants' nests and not full of poisonous snakes and spiders. Stockpile some canned meat. Maybe make amends with that gang of ornery survivalists you offended by saying you were an advocate of tighter gun control. Then deploy the Square Lashing to turn that campsite into something a little more homely.

The Square Lashing is a full-on load-bearing knot for joining two poles together, generally at a right angle. It's very useful for building impromptu scaffolding, and with experience could be used with poles at a 45-degree angle as well.

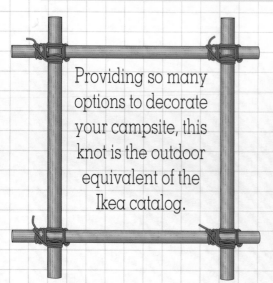

Providing so many options to decorate your campsite, this knot is the outdoor equivalent of the Ikea catalog.

1 While the knot described here is between only two poles, it is designed to hold four together, with a binding at each crossing. So begin by laying two poles down parallel to each other, and laying two more poles on top of these, crossing at their ends at right angles. At any one of the four right-angle crossings, begin by tying a simple Clove Hitch (Lesson 18) to the pole that is underneath.

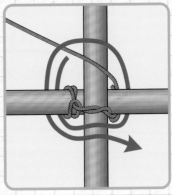

2 Twist the short end around the long working end. Bring the twisted end over the pole that is lying on top. Now bring that twist under the pole that is underneath, then back over the top pole.

3 Now go back under (this should involve crossing where your initial clove hitch was), and then back over. Repeat this over-and-under process three or four times, making sure to end on one of the turns that goes over the top pole.

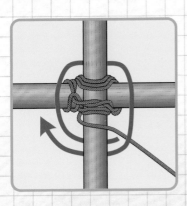

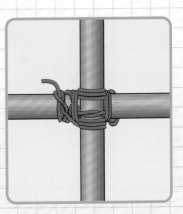

4 Now bring the rope back around the center lashing. Pass it under the top pole and back over the underneath pole, effectively wrapping the lashing. Repeat this three or four times. (This is known as a frapping turn, and it adds security to a lashing at right angles.)

5 Finish the binding with two or three Half Hitches (Lesson 2) on the pole that lies underneath.

Tripod Lashing
A knot for campfire cooks

Any self-respecting knot adventurer has to have a much-dented cooking pot to contain their vast array of instant noodles and/or healing tinctures. Where there's a fine old cooking pot, there's got to be a big old fire. And where there's a fire, there ought to be three sticks lashed together from which the aforementioned pot can hang.

This is useful for many a job. A single Tripod Lashing can be used to hold a container for a makeshift basin; or make two to support a pole for spit-roasting a chicken or something larger. You could even use four knots to build the legs for a makeshift table.

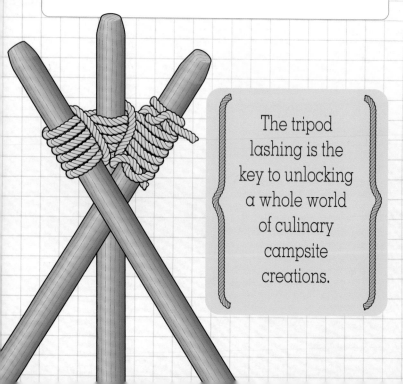

The tripod lashing is the key to unlocking a whole world of culinary campsite creations.

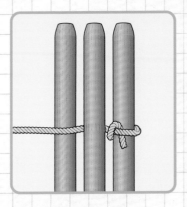

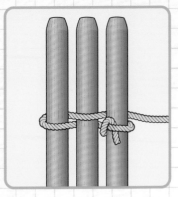

1 Put the three poles next to one another with about ½ in. (1 cm) between them. Tie a Half Hitch (Lesson 2) on one of the outer poles. Bring the long working end under the middle pole, then over the third pole.

2 Now bring it back over the middle pole and under the first pole. You're creating a woven effect known as "racking turns." This is designed to reduce slipping.

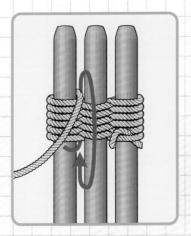

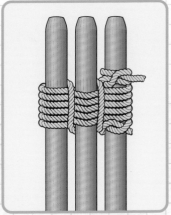

3 Continue making racking turns until you have five or six around all the poles. Now make two frapping turns (see page 53) in each of the two gaps.

4 Finish with a Clove Hitch (Lesson 18). Cross the two outside poles over each other to form up the tripod.

Celtic Knot

A knot to enjoy with a pint of Guinness

It's been a long, hard day in the Forest of Infinite Despair (and Stuff), and it's time to tuck into some hard-earned raccoon stew. But that steaming heap of protein is hot! This looks like a job for some sort of decorative mat. Go ahead, say that aloud, it'll make you giggle: "This looks like a job for some sort of decorative mat!" We're silly.

✹ There are infinite permutations of the traditional Celtic Knot; what follows is a very basic version. If you're developing an affinity for knots (which is likely if you've made it this far through the book), it can be great fun to start exploring the rich world of decorative knots. This works best with your rope lying on a flat surface. Keep the rope loose while you make your turns.

1 Begin by creating a small bight (see page 5) at one end of the rope. Pass the other end under the rope and then over the first end, leaving a loop behind. The over/under sequence will continue throughout this knot.

2 Bring the long working end back around toward the first loop. Pass over it, then under it.

3 Pass the end through the second loop, going over the rope, then under it. Then pass it over the matching loop on the other side, and under it. The working end of the rope should now be at the bottom of the pretzel shape you've formed.

4 Now follow the original strand all the way back through, following the same over-and-under sequence, ending at the starting position.

5 You can continue this pattern either until you are pleased with how it looks or until you run out of rope. To keep a nice appearance, you'll want to "hide" the final turn by tucking it in. The ropes can be pulled tight, and if you want to finish the piece, a few methods can be used. If the ends will melt, you can use flame, although kids should get an adult to help. Glue or a needle and thread are also options, as is a Constrictor Knot (Lesson 22). Whatever you choose, be mindful that you should keep the finishes hidden.

A Handy Guide to Climbing In and Out of All the Things
(climbing knots)

Your knot-tying prowess has conquered the forest and the ocean, but it's time to get real and climb higher. Literally. It's time to go into full-on mountaineer mode.

The life of the knot-tier is fraught with danger and delight, but for some reason, no matter how great your prowess, you always end up climbing over, on top of, and out of stuff. So ready yourself, intrepid knot adventurer, because Danger is calling, and she doesn't like to leave a message after the tone. Of danger!

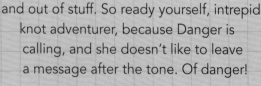
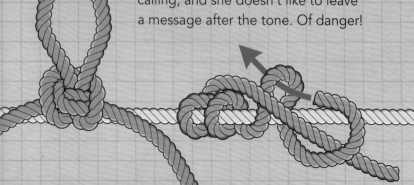

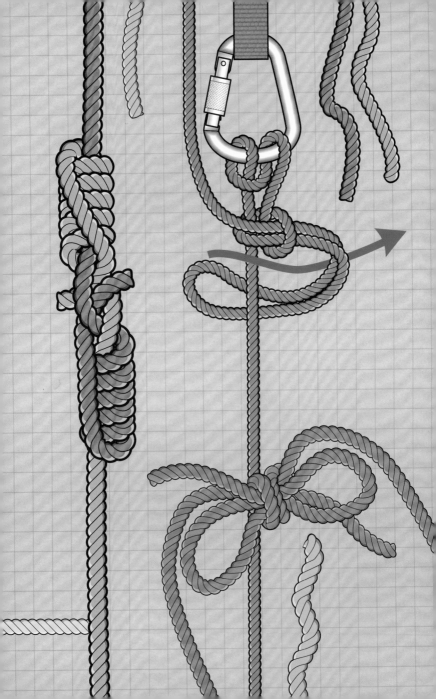

Bow Tie
A knot for the dapper gent

While not strictly necessary for climbing, the bow tie is critical for you to sport after you've climbed the peak of the previously insurmountable mountain. You see, once you reach those heady heights, all the world's press are going to want a piece of you, and so it's important to look your best. And what says "Hey, I just climbed a mountain that's more dangerous than telling a group of fanatical One Direction fans that their latest single sucks" more than a neatly tied bow tie?

1 Look in a mirror. You look nice. Set the tie up on your neck such that there is a long and a short side. As a right-hander, I prefer to have the long end hanging on my right.

2 Bring the long over the short, then tuck it under the short end and pull it tight.

3 Now take the dangling short end and fold it into a little bow, just like the shape of half a bow tie, keeping it in place with your fingers.

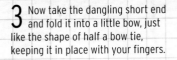

4 Bring the long end down over your folded half bow. The bulk of the standing end is going to become the center of your bow tie.

5 This last step is the one that takes some practice. It requires you to have faith in your hands, since it's the hardest to see. Fold the long end into and behind the small bow. You want to pass it behind the front bow, but not so much that you pull it all the way through. Hopefully tighten and straighten, or else untie and start again in frustration. Don't lose your cool, Mountain Man.

Lark's Head (or Cow Hitch, Lanyard Hitch)

A knot for a quick hitch

Your climbing partner has stepped on the wrong patch of ice, and you hear that haunting creaking sound. You know an avalanche is imminent and you need to tie a hitch in a hurry. Sure, you could use the good old clove hitch, but why not try out another, equally unreliable hitch for a change? I can see no reason why you wouldn't.

This is essentially a Clove (Lesson 18) with the second turn reversed. It's a really fast and easy hitch, and in some ways it is more reliable than the clove, as it usually feels a bit less likely to bind on you. But, also like the clove, it shouldn't be relied on by itself. It's also useful with smaller ropes and lines (it's a popular method for attaching kites), and can be extended into a decorative knot with a cocktail of passion and finesse.

1 Bring the working end of the rope around the object or another rope, and bring it back around itself.

2 Now bring it back around the object or other rope in the reverse direction and pull it down beside itself.

Munter Mule and Hitch

A knot for escaping an avalanche

You survived Lesson 30, but your lead-legged buddy has only done it again. As you sprint past a Yeti and a guy named Stew (poor Stew), you find your path blocked by a huge cliff. You see a sign stating "DANGER—risk of avalanche," and some quick thinking turns this object into an escape route. You throw a lightning-fast Munter around the signpost and launch yourself to freedom. Very cool.

✱ This reliable climbing hitch works well for a controlled descent using only rope and a locking carabiner—that hook-thingy that is used most often with climbing gear, but equally often to hold the keys of rugged and cool people.

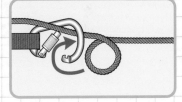

1 Bring the rope into the body of the carabiner. Form a loop on the rope above where you've passed it into the carabiner, and then hook that loop onto the mouth of the open carabiner.

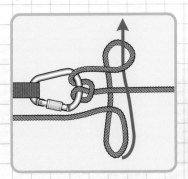

2 Now form two more medium-sized loops above the carabiner and use them to tie a Slip Knot (Lesson 10). Leave a long loop at the end of the slip knot.

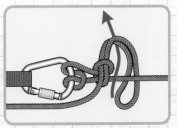

3 Use this large loop to finish the knot with a Half Hitch (Lesson 2), bringing the loop around the climbing rope and under itself.

Alpine Butterfly Loop
A knot for a makeshift zipline

Here we are again: it's your annual ski trip and a snowstorm has set in, shutting down the ski lift and leaving you stranded at the top of the Olympic downhill run… for the third time this week. To escape the fate of becoming a human snowman, you must cheat death by attaching your rope to the lift cable and quickly sliding to safety. Don't look down, and most certainly don't squeal "Wheeeeeeeee!" as you go.

It's true, this is a solid knot for making a loop in the middle of a rope. It has a variety of practical uses, often while climbing or camping. This specific variant owes a nod to the amazing creators of animatedknots.com, as their technique is a significant improvement on other forms in terms of helping you find the loop. It seems and feels complicated to explain, but it can become second-nature with a little practice, and is a very good knot indeed to know.

Fun fact: make this loop at night-time and it's known as the Alpine Moth.

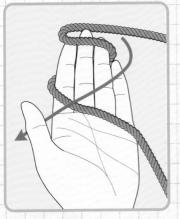

1 With your palm facing upward, do two turns of the rope around your hand, ending the second turn at your fingertips.

2 Finish the second turn by bringing the rope back toward your thumb, such that you have a loop above your index finger and an "X" at the top of your palm.

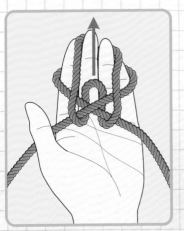

3 Now take the loop that has formed above your fingertips and pull it over and around the other turn (or the "X" in your palm).

4 Bring the formed-up knot off your hand. Tighten it and form up the loop by pulling the loop and both the ends.

Double Alpine Butterfly Loop

A knot for two makeshift ziplines

The Double Alpine is just like the Alpine, but with two more turns, adding another loop. It can be just as useful to know as the regular version, and is worth noting in itself as the need for one loop often leads to the need for still another. Loop greed. It runs rampant in the climber community.

1 Make four turns of the rope around your hand, ending the second and third turns at your fingertips. Finish the fourth turn by bringing the rope back toward your thumb, such that you have a loop above your index finger and an "X" at the top of your palm.

2 Now take the two loops that have formed near your fingertips and pull them over and around the other turn (or the "X" in your palm).

3 Bring the formed-up knot off your hand. Tighten it and form up the two loops by pulling the loops and both the ends.

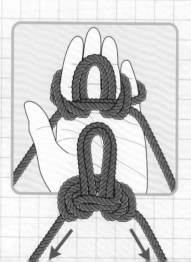

Prusik Knot
A knot for safe climbing

Not all climbing happens on mountains; caves, canyons, cliffs, and climbing walls also offer fun vertical opportunities. One thing these spots have in common is that the Prusik is your key to safety. Plus a harness. And a rope. And some more rope. And a climbing partner and a carabiner. You have all that stuff, right?

✳ Use this knot for ascending or rescue missions. It doesn't damage the rope it is attached to, despite its strong hold. Skilled climbers use two Prusiks in tandem to climb mountains.

1 Begin with one rope already tied into a loop using the Double Fisherman's Knot (Lesson 15). We'll be attaching the first rope to another rope, usually a wider one. Form a loop on the opposite end of the fisherman's knot, with the thicker rope passing over it.

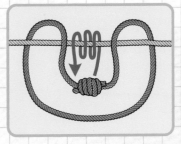

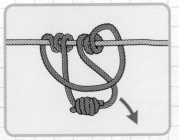

2 Pass the knot through the loop and make three turns around the rope you are tying it to.

3 After the third turn, pass the knot through the loop, making sure the turns have lined up neatly next to one another. Pull the knot tight.

Better Bow

A knot for shoelace perfectionists

With all your mountaineering equipment lost in the ascent of Maiden's Peak, you find yourself once again careening down a mountain at full bore, tearing through a jungle with a group of rock-tossing locals in close pursuit. You don't speak the local lingo, but it seems likely that they are saying either friendly things about your feet or unfriendly things about your mother. Good thing you know that your trusted climbing shoes won't betray you, since they've been tied with the Better Bow! Maybe you will take that sponsorship deal from them after all?

Most of us know how to tie our shoelaces, but, as with so much of life, it can be both confusing and exhilarating to dissect this hardwired process. Moreover, there are a few things we don't automatically realize. One is that a shoelace knot is essentially an Overhand Knot (Lesson 1!) with two big bows. Fine, you knew that, but did you also know that there is a better way to double-tie than retying the bow? Well, then skip this, smart ass!

Did you know, the average person ties their shoelaces over 10,000 times during their lifetime.*

* This is a completely made-up statistic.

1 Start as normal when tying your shoes, forming an overhand knot and making a loop.

2 Now, instead of making the next turn right into the next loop, wrap the first with two full turns. Wrap these two turns around your finger, as you would with a typical shoe-tying experience.

3 Form a second loop and push it through the opening you've made with your finger.

4 Pull the loops! It really does work better, and can be used with equal assurance on any variety of bathing apparel.

Blood Knot

A knot that sounds pretty darn cool

This is another method for joining two ropes that happens to be pretty effective. It is best suited to yelling out loud, in the face of a fellow climber who's trying to show off. As in, "I'll take care of that with a simple Blood Knot...you jackass!"

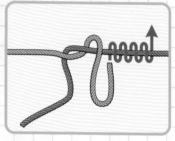

2 Bring one line around the other for at least five turns. The more turns, the stronger the knot.

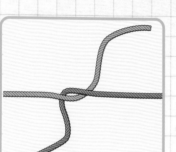

1 Overlap the two lines.

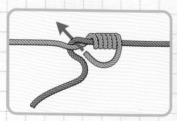

3 Now tuck that end over the turns and between the overlap in the two lines.

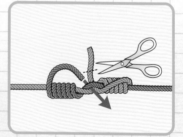

4 Mirror this in the other direction with the other line, wrapping for five to seven turns and bringing the end back through. Pull both tight and trim up any excess.

> The Blood Knot is a straightforward and effective way to join two lines.

Sheep Shank
A knot that's good for nothing

You're out for a stroll on Hood Mountain, taking in the sights. Spruce tree here, big rock there. Hey look, it's the Infinite Abyss. You've been meaning to check that out. If only you knew a safe shortening knot to use for diving in and exploring just a bit.

And some would say that the Sheep Shank falls short of that. It's notorious because so many people have had to learn it, most conspicuously as a Scout requirement. Many discerning knot-smiths look on this knot with disdain, but it's a curiosity if only for its popularity compared to its ineffectiveness. In a way, it makes sense that it is popular, as it is rather fun to tie.

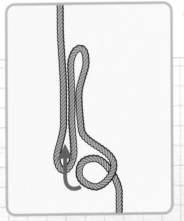

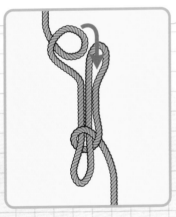

1 Fold the rope over on itself to the new length, creating two bights (see page 5) alternating in each direction. Form a Half Hitch (Lesson 2) in one of the standing ends of one of the bights, and bring it over the adjacent bight. Tighten.

2 Repeat on the opposite side, forming up another half hitch and bringing it over the bight. Tighten. Now don't use this for anything.

The Knut

A knot for people who failed high-school English

While tricky to tie, this knot is uniquely self-advancing. It lends itself to a more leisurely upward-scaling of an otherwise impenetrable cliff, in case you've left your cool suction-cup climbing thingies at home.

1 Make a bight (see page 5) in the rope, just underneath your line. Make a turn over and around the line, keeping the bight at the bottom in place.

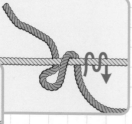

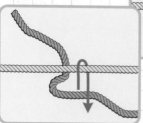

2 Make an additional three turns, giving you four in total.

3 Take the working end that is heading upward and bring it back around the turns toward the bight, effectively making one turn around the turns.

4 Bring the working end back up and through the bottom-most bight, and pull tight.

Scaffold Knot

A knot to use if you plan to be suspended above deadly animals

A stronger alternative to the Poacher's Knot (Lesson 21), this noose can be used to create a secure foothold if you're dangling above a pit of hungry alligators.

1 Form a loop at the end of the rope. Bring the working end back toward the loop.

2 Make three turns as you bring the working end toward the loop, keeping the wraps a little loose.

3 Bring the working end back through the turns and pull tight.

The Knot Tier's Guide to Escape

(miscellaneous strong knots and tying diversions)

From Houdini to Bond, many great people had even greater escapes. Whether fleeing from trouble or hurtling into the jaws of it, knot know-how is the thing to have in a tight spot.

Mooring Hitch

A knot for hanging things (or mooring things)

If your backpack has been suspended high above you, with a simple tug this quick-release knot will send it tumbling into your arms.

The Mooring Hitch is another quick and effective hitch. Like so many hitches before it, it isn't terribly reliable, but it can be used for a quick tie-up.

1 Bring the rope over a pole, and make a loop in the working end that lies against the standing end.

2 Make a small bight (see page 5) in the working end and pass it over the loop, under the standing end, and back over the loop.

3 Tighten the hitch to secure the bight in place.

Highwayman's Hitch

A knot that gives you an excuse to say "your money or your life!"

As the name indicates, this knot was popular with thieves and brigands, who used it for escaping after a heist.

✳ This is another fairly useful hitch, mostly worth noting because of its very cool name.

1 Hold a bight (see page 5) against a pole. Bring a second bight behind the pole and then around the first.

2 Form up still another little bight on the tail of the working end. Bring the last bight through the first.

3 Pull tight. Pull the tail if you want a quick release.

Running Bowline
A knot for reuniting you with lost gadgets

The Running Bowline is a kind of non-binding noose. Say it's your Grandma's birthday, but you haven't called her yet to say "Happy birthday," and you drop your phone into an unreachable crevasse. Send this fellow in to retrieve it and go on to make Granny's day.

✴ This is a valuable variant on the Bowline (Lesson 17), and it can be used in many settings.

> The running bowline—keeping Grannies happy, since the invention of the cell phone.

1 Bring the rope over a pole or branch. Form a loop in the working end tail.

2 Bring the working end behind the standing end, then through the loop.

3 Now bring the end back around itself and back through the loop to form up your old friend the Bowline (Lesson 17).

4 Pull the standing end to run the bowline up against the pole.

Package Knot

A knot for big packages *snigger*

Best for keeping safe any items you wish to send to your fellow knot adventurers—whether it's a new length of rope or a copy of this awesome knot book that you just have to share.

This is an ideal knot for making your packages look extra fancy, while also making certain the contents remain where they should.

1 First form up a standard Slip Knot and Noose (Lesson 10), large enough to fit around the package with some excess. Bring it around the package and tighten it, leaving a long working end.

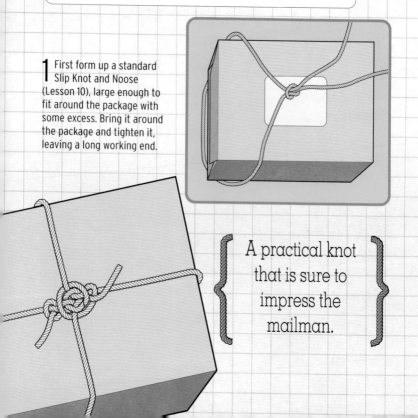

A practical knot that is sure to impress the mailman.

2 Flip the package over. Bring the long working end over the rope of the tightened noose. Then bring that end back over the tightened noose, leaving a small bight (see page 5) behind. Now bring it under the noose rope and over the bight and tighten.

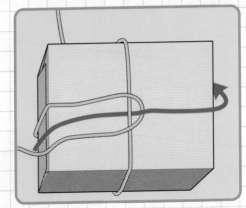

3 Flip the package over. Bring the working end under and then over the four strands surrounding the noose knot, alternating all the way round.

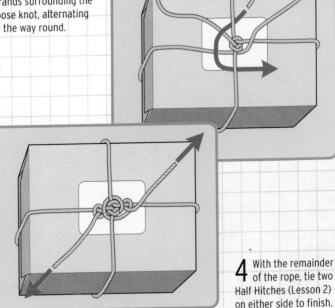

4 With the remainder of the rope, tie two Half Hitches (Lesson 2) on either side to finish.

Barrel Hitch

A knot for lifting barrels

Oh no! What was supposed to be a fun hike in the forest has suddenly taken a turn for the worse. You and your buddy managed to disturb a particularly angry hermit, and have had to flee. Luckily, ol' Herman realized three was a crowd and quickly retreated, but not before your friend sprained his ankle. How are you going to get him across this gulch with only hope, a rope, and a handy barrel that someone has helpfully left by the cliff edge?

This is how you safely tie a rope around a barrel. You're on your own for the remainder of the rescue mission.

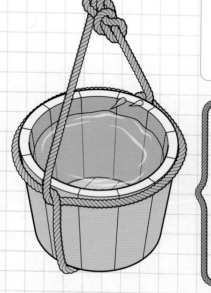

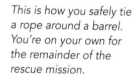

Tie this hitch around a drinks can and attach it to the arm of your chair. Hey presto... Instant cup holder!

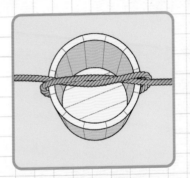

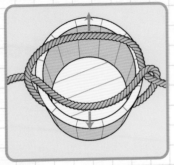

1 Tie an Overhand Knot (Lesson 1) across the top of a barrel, wrapping the knot around the body of the barrel. (Essentially you are tying one big overhand knot with a barrel in the middle of it.)

2 Spread the ropes of the overhand out such that they wrap around the mouth of the barrel.

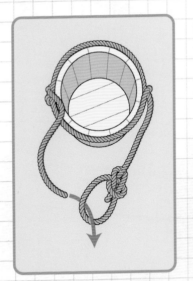

3 Join the ends with a Bowline (Lesson 17).

4 Lift the barrel upward in order to finish the knot.

Trucker's Hitch

A knot for those who like to keep on truckin'

This is a mighty one. It's best for securing a really large piece of cargo—given the name, probably a large truck, or an even larger trucker—to a really big, rickety wagon.

> *Make sure your bike, dog, piano, wardrobe, bed, or cherished collection of knots stay in place with this extra-secure hitch.*

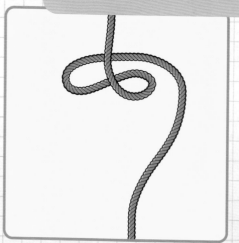

1 Form a bight (see page 5), then make a figure eight around the standing end by bringing the bight around the rope and leaving a small loop behind.

2 Pass the bight back over the rope and down through the open loop. (You can also use a Bowline, Lesson 17, or Alpine Butterfly Loop, Lesson 32, here.)

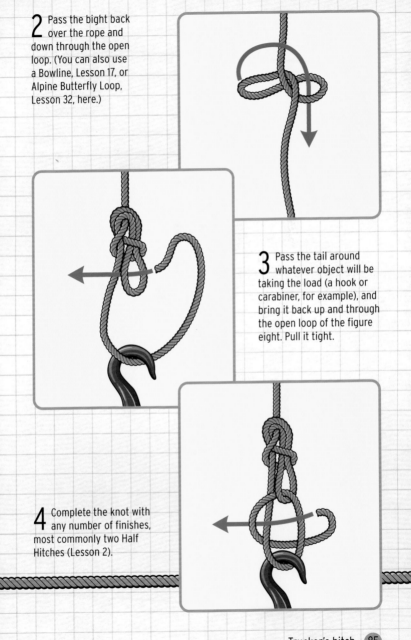

3 Pass the tail around whatever object will be taking the load (a hook or carabiner, for example), and bring it back up and through the open loop of the figure eight. Pull it tight.

4 Complete the knot with any number of finishes, most commonly two Half Hitches (Lesson 2).

Honda Knot (or Lasso)

A knot for lovers of Japanese cars and Lonesome cowboys

Life on the range can be lonely for a cowboy, so why not seek the company of a friendly-looking cow to shoot the breeze with? Simply tie the Honda Knot and lasso the steer over for an evening of beers and conversation about sports. This heifer's a big fan of both the Dallas Cowboys and the Chicago Bulls.

> The essential go-to for a cowboy on the go, this is best used to lasso herds of cattle.

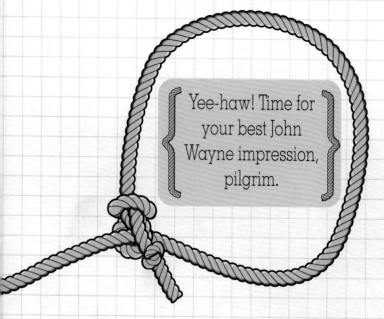

Yee-haw! Time for your best John Wayne impression, pilgrim.

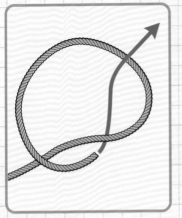

1 Tie a loose Overhand Knot (Lesson 1) close to the end of your rope.

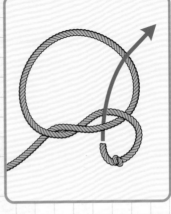

2 Tie a tight overhand knot at the very end of the rope, as a stopper knot. Bring the tightened overhand knot through the loose one.

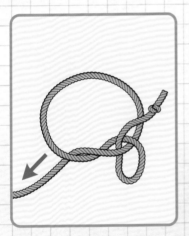

3 Pull the standing end to tighten the loose overhand knot. You've formed up a perfectly circular Honda Knot.

4 Bring the main line back through the Honda to form a lasso of any size. Being a traditional knot, this is intended for use with very stiff rope.

Handcuff Knot
A knot for crime-fighters

CREAK! What was that? You wake in the night and hear movement. Your eyes adjust to the gloom and you reach for the nearest object you can find: a trusty rope. You creep out the bedroom and see the unmistakable silhouette of a man. Quick as a flash you pounce, with no thought for your own safety, and tie his hands together with the Handcuff Knot. Take that, thief! Except it's not a thief, it's your poor roommate getting a glass of water. D'oh!

Whether you need to capture an irritated Yeti or a burglar, this mightiest of all handcuffs will never fail you. Actually, it probably will, but it's fun to make handcuffs out of rope.

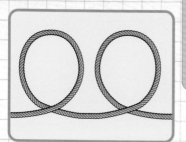

1 Make two loops of the same size in the rope.

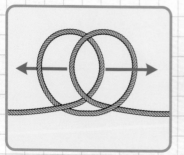

2 Overlap them half over each other.

3 Bring each loop through the other loop. Pull tight.

Tumble Hitch

A knot for acrobats and cowboys in a hurry

You know those scenes in Westerns where a cowboy jumps on his horse and rides away instantly into the sunset while the pursuing sheriff wonders how he untied his horse so quickly? No? Just me, then. Anyway…humor me and imagine that scene. This knot would be great there, allowing the cowboy to untie his steed in an instant.

✳ This final hitch is the most reliable of the quick-release hitches. I was holding out all along.

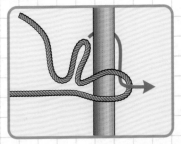

1 Bring a bight (see page 5) against a pole. Make a second little bight under the first, and bring it through the first bight.

2 Bring the working end around the standing end, then form up a third bight in the working end and bring it through the second bight.

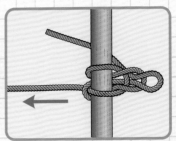

3 Tighten the standing end to secure the load. Pull the tail to release.

Make a Net

A knot for knot obsessives

Who doesn't need a net? Well, most people who don't have to regularly capture their own dinner. This transcends knot-tying and becomes an intensive hobby of its own, but you'll be glad you forgot how to do this once you're trapped on a deserted island after the Apocalypse.

Yes, it may seem complicated, and yes, it is time-consuming, but this is a satisfying task to undertake because, whether it's a fish or a thief in the night, you never know when you'll need a net to catch something.

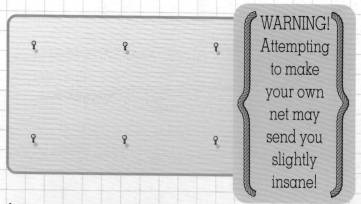

WARNING! Attempting to make your own net may send you slightly insane!

1 There are a variety of knots that can be used as the so-called net knot, which joins each of the cells of the net, but we suggest the Sheet Bend (Lesson 8). If you end up needing to add rope, use a Fisherman's Knot (Lesson 15).

While this can be done free-form, we suggest building a peg board as a working guide. Lay out a board with nails in place for each corner of each net cell. They should be even and to the desired size of your net.

2 Using the guides, bring a length of rope around the four corners of the first cell and tie a sheet bend tightly around the first nail that you have brought the rope back to.

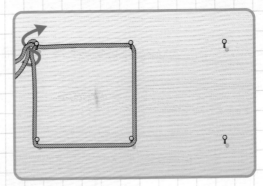

3 Double back to the second nail, and tie another sheet bend to ready yourself to move to the next cell.

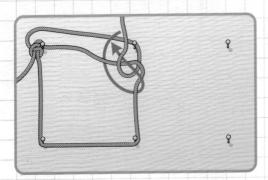

4 Make another cell, finishing and tying at what is effectively the bottom right-hand corner of your first cell, or the corner below the knot you just tied. Repeat this until you get to the edge, then begin working in the next direction until finished.

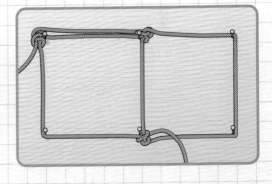

Monkey Braid

A knot for when things get a bit too much

{ Because monkeys also like to get their hair did }

You've been stuck on this desert island for a few days now. You've drunk all the duty-free booze you bought; it's too hot; and you've got sand in your sleeping bag. Frankly, you're getting a bit fed up. You need something to help you relax a bit, and that's where the Monkey Braid comes in.

Last, and potentially least, is a useless decorative knot. It can be fun and distracting, though.

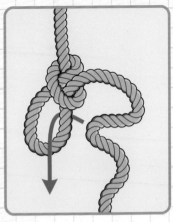

1 Make a small, loose noose somewhere on the rope. Form a bight (see page 5) close to the noose and tuck it back into the loop of the noose.

2 Make another bight and tuck it into the previous noose.

3 Repeat this for as long as you like, or until you are out of rope.

4 You can tighten the braid by passing the end through the final loop, or you can "magically" untie it by pulling both ends.

Index